A Grain of Mustard Seed

New Poems

Books by May Sarton

A Grain of Mustard Seed

New Poems
By MAY SARTON

W · W · NORTON & COMPANY

New York · London

The author wishes to thank the editors of the following journals, where some of these poems made their first appearance: *Ante, Contempora, Friends Journal, The Green River Review, The Ladies' Home Journal, The Lyric, The Massachusetts Review, The New Yorker, Poetry, The Saturday Review, The Small Pond, Twigs, United Church Herald, The Virginia Quarterly Review, Voices, Yankee.*

W. W. Norton & Company, Inc., 500 Fifth Avenue, New York, NY 10110
W. W. Norton & Company Ltd., 10 Coptic Street London WC1A 1PU

PRINTED IN THE UNITED STATES OF AMERICA

ISBN 0-393-04344-4

2 3 4 5 6 7 8 9 0

TO

M. H. H.

Contents

Part One

BALLAD OF THE SIXTIES

In the West of the country where I was
Hoping for some good news,
Only the cripple had fire,
Only the cripple knew the mind's desire;
In the wheel chair alone
Poetry met the eyes
That see and recognize,
There in the wizened bone.
> For only the ill are well,
> And only the mad are sane.
> This is the sad truth plain,
> The story I have to tell.

In the North of the country where I saw
The anxious rich and the angry poor,
Only the blasted life had reason;
Only the stricken in the bitter season
Looked out of loss and learned
The waste of all that burned,
Once cared and burned.
> For only the mad are sane,
> And only the lost are well,
> And loss of fire the bane
> Of this season in Hell.

In the South of the country where I passed
Looking for faith and hope at last,
Only the black man knew
The false dream from the true;
Only the dark and grieving
Could be the still believing.
> For only the ill are well,
> Only the hunted, free,
> So the story I have to tell
> In the South was told to me.

] 11 [

In the East of the country where I came
Back to my house, back to my name,
Only the crazy girl was clear
That all has been betrayed to fear;
Only the mad girl knew the cost,
And she, shut up from wind and rain
And safely plucked out from her pain,
Knew that our love is lost, is lost.
       For only the sick are well;
       The mad alone have truth to tell
       In the mad games they play—
       Our love has withered away.

THE ROCK IN THE SNOWBALL
(for Mark Howe)

How little I knew you, Mark, to mourn so wild
As if death hit square in the mouth today.
That snowball held a rock and it hurt hard.
But even outraged, am I still a child
To take death with raw grief and howl my way
Hand against mouth to ward off the word?

How little I knew you, Mark, but for the blue
Those deep-set eyes shafted across a room
To prick the ghost of pride or of pretence,
That straight look into doom if it were true,
That poker look that made our laughter bloom
And burned up sham like paper with a glance.

You were exposed, a man stripped down to care,
Thin as a boy, tempest-torn as a boy,
And sick with pity, conscience-caught-and-bound.
Courage is easy—every boy can dare—
But harder to keep justice from that joy,
And bury feeling, your self-inflicted wound.

And yet you burned. And yet you burned so deep,
Mastering fire, controlling fire with wit,
That eulogies seem pale beside your breath,
And we are fools, since you would not, to weep.
We mourn ourselves, that is the truth of it,
Hit by the savage rock that is your death.

Whatever end we hoped with you alive,
To be those few, and happy, growing old,
To talk of battles shared, of false and true,
That light is gone. We shall have to survive
As remnants in a world turned grim and cold
Where once we laughed at Hell itself with you.

] 13 [

THE BALLAD OF RUBY *

Her mother dressed the child in white,
White ribbons plaited in her hair,
And sent her off to school to fight
Though it was very cruel there.
"Ruby, we have to show our pride.
Walk slow, and just be dignified."

So Ruby walked to school each day
While the white mothers screamed "Black scum!"
Never got dirty out at play
For she spent recess in her room,
And felt the hatred seeping in.
"What is it, mother? What have I done?"

But still her mother had to trust
That that white dress so clean and neat
Would show the truth because it must,
Her Ruby was so bright and sweet.
And every day the crowd grew bigger
And threw stones at the "dirty nigger."

Then Ruby shook her ribboned head,
Refused to eat a chocolate cookie,
Had nightmares every night in bed,
Broke her brown crayons—"They are mucky!
"Ugly is black. Ugly is last."
(Ruby at six was learning fast).

And when the teacher let them draw,
Ruby made all black people lame,
White people tall, strong, without flaw.
Her drawing did not need a name.
"It is plain black and white, you see.
And black is ugly. Black is me."

* The story of Ruby is told by Robert Coles in *Children of Crisis*, Atlantic Monthly Press, 1967.

"We'll poison you" became the taunt.
"You'll learn to keep away from white!"
And so a new fear came to haunt
The child who had no appetite,
Locked into blackness like some sin.
"Why mother? Is it *only* my skin?"

But still she walked to school with glory,
And ran the gauntlet, dignified. . . .
Did she grow up to tell a different story?—
"White folks are black, all dirty down inside.
What makes them like they are, ugly within?
Is it *only* the color of their skin?"

THE BALLAD OF JOHNNY
(*A News Item*)

For safety on the expedition
A name-tag on each child was hung,
A necklace-name, his very own,
So he could not get lost for long.

Johnny jumped up and down for joy
To have a name forever true.
"I'm Johnny," cried the little boy.
"Johnny is going to the zoo!"

"Johnny," he whispered in the subway.
His whole face was suffused with bliss.
This was the best, the greatest day.
Boldly he gave his name a kiss.

But soon forgot it at the zoo
And let the name-tag swing out free,
For could that elephant be true?
And there was so much there to see . . .

Look, Johnny, at the monkey swinging
High in the air on his trapeze!
He heard the gibbon's sharp shrill singing
And begged to hold the monkey, please.

Then saw a goat and ran off fast
To hug the dear fantastic thing,
An animal to stroke at last,
A living toy for all his loving.

The soft lips nibbled at his sweater
And Johnny laughed with joy to feel
Such new-found friendliness and, better,
To know this animal was real.

His face was breathing in fur coat,
He did not notice anything
As gentle lips and greedy throat
Swallowed the name-tag and the string.

But when he found that they were gone
And he had lost his name for good,
Dreadful it was to be alone,
And Johnny screamed his terror loud.

The friendly goat was strange and wild,
And the cold eyes' indifferent stare
Could give no comfort to the child
Who had become No one, Nowhere.

"I've lost my name. I'm going to die,"
He shouted when his teacher came
And found him too afraid to cry.
"But, Johnny, you still have your name!

"It's not a tag, it's in your head,
And you are Johnny through and through.
Look in the mirror," teacher said,
"There's Johnny looking out at you."

But he had never had a mirror,
And Johnny met there a strange child
And screamed dismay at this worse error,
And only grew more lost and wild.

"No, no," he screamed, "that is not me,
That ugly boy I don't know who . . ."
Great treasure lost, identity,
When a goat ate it at the zoo.

EASTER, 1968

Now we have buried the face we never knew,
Now we have silenced the voice we never heard,
Now he is dead we look on him with awe . . .
Dead king, dear martyr, and anointed Word.
Where thousands followed, each must go home
Into his secret heart and learn the pain,
Stand there on rock and, utterly alone,
Come to terms with this burning suffering man;
Torn by his hunger from our fat and greed,
And bitten by his thirst from careless sloth,
Must wake, inflamed, to answer for his blood
With the slow-moving inexorable truth
That we can earn even a moment's balm
Only with acts of caring, and fierce calm.

Head of an African, vital and young,
The full lips fervent as an open rose,
The high-domed forehead full of light and strong—
Look on this man again. The blood still flows.
Listen once more to the impassioned voice
Till we are lifted on his golden throat
And trumpet-call of agony and choice
Out of our hesitating shame and doubt.
Remember how he prayed before the task.
Remember how he walked, eyes bright and still,
Unarmed, his bronze face shining like a mask,
Through stones and curses, hatred hard as hail.
Now we have silenced the voice we never heard,
Break open, heart, and listen to his word.

THE INVOCATION TO KALI

"... the Black Goddess Kali, the terrible one of many names, 'difficult of approach,' whose stomach is a void and so can never be filled, and whose womb is giving birth forever to all things ..." Joseph Campbell, *The Masks of God: Oriental Mythology*, The Viking Press, Inc. 1962, p. 5.

1

There are times when
I think only of killing
The voracious animal
Who is my perpetual shame,

The violent one
Whose raging demands
Break down peace and shelter
Like a peacock's scream.

There are times when
I think only of how to do away
With this brute power
That cannot be tamed.

I am the cage where poetry
Paces and roars. The beast
Is the god. How murder the god?
How live with the terrible god?

2

The Kingdom of Kali

Anguish is always there, lurking at night,
Wakes us like a scourge, the creeping sweat
As rage is remembered, self-inflicted blight.
What is it in us we have not mastered yet?

What Hell have we made of the subtle weaving
Of nerve with brain, that all centers tear?
We live in a dark complex of rage and grieving.
The machine grates, grates, whatever we are.

The kingdom of Kali is within us deep.
The built-in destroyer, the savage goddess,
Wakes in the dark and takes away our sleep.
She moves through the blood to poison gentleness.

She keeps us from being what we long to be;
Tenderness withers under her iron laws.
We may hold her like a lunatic, but it is she
Held down, who bloodies with her claws.

How then to set her free or come to terms
With the volcano itself, the fierce power
Erupting injuries, shrieking alarms?
Kali among her skulls must have her hour.

It is time for the invocation, to atone
For what we fear most and have not dared to face:
Kali, the destroyer, cannot be overthrown;
We must stay, open-eyed, in the terrible place.

Every creation is born out of the dark.
Every birth is bloody. Something gets torn.
Kali is there to do her sovereign work
Or else the living child will be still-born.

She cannot be cast out (she is here for good)
Nor battled to the end. Who wins that war?
She cannot be forgotten, jailed, or killed.
Heaven must still be balanced against her.

Out of destruction she comes to wrest
The juice from the cactus, its harsh spine,
And until she, the destroyer, has been blest,
There will be no child, no flower, and no wine.

3

The Concentration Camps

Have we managed to fade them out like God?
Simply eclipse the unpurged images?
Eclipse the children with a mountain of shoes?
Let the bones fester like animal bones,

] 20 [

False teeth, bits of hair, spilled liquid eyes,
Disgusting, not to be looked at, like a blight?

Ages ago we closed our hearts to blight.
Who believes now? Who cries, "merciful God"?
We gassed God in the ovens, great piteous eyes,
Burned God in a trash-heap of images,
Refused to make a compact with dead bones,
And threw away the children with their shoes—

Millions of sandals, sneakers, small worn shoes—
Thrust them aside as a disgusting blight.
Not ours, this death, to take into our bones,
Not ours a dying mutilated God.
We freed our minds from gruesome images,
Pretended we had closed their open eyes

That never could be closed, dark puzzled eyes,
The ghosts of children who went without shoes
Naked toward the ovens' bestial images,
Strangling for breath, clawing the blight,
Piled up like pigs beyond the help of God. . . .
With food in our stomachs, flesh on our bones,

We turned away from the stench of bones,
Slept with the living, drank in sexy eyes,
Hurried for shelter from a murdered God.
New factories turned out millions of shoes.
We hardly noticed the faint smell of blight,
Stuffed with new cars, ice cream, rich images.

But no grass grew on the raw images.
Corruption mushroomed from decaying bones.
Joy disappeared. The creature of the blight
Rose in the cities, dark smothered eyes.
Our children danced with rage in their shoes,
Grew up to question who had murdered God,

While we evaded their too attentive eyes,
Walked the pavane of death in our new shoes,
Sweated with anguish and remembered God.

The Time of Burning

For a long time we shall have only to listen,
Not argue or defend, but listen to each other.
Let curses fall without intercession,
Let those fires burn we have tried to smother.

What we have pushed aside and tried to bury
Lives with a staggering thrust we cannot parry.

We have to reckon with Kali for better or worse,
The angry tongue that lashes us with flame
As long-held hope turns bitter and men curse,
"Burn, baby, burn" in the goddess' name.

We are asked to bear it, to take in the whole,
The long indifferent beating down of soul.

It is the time of burning, hate exposed.
We shall have to live with only Kali near.
She comes in her fury, early or late, disposed
To tantrums we have earned and must endure.

We have to listen to the harsh undertow
To reach the place where Kali can bestow.

But she must have her dreadful empire first
Until the prisons of the mind are broken free
And every suffering center at its worst
Can be appealed to her dark mystery.

She comes to purge the altars in her way,
And at her altar we shall have to pray.

It is a place of skulls, a deathly place
Where we confront our violence and feel,
Before that broken and self-ravaged face,
The murderers we are, brought here to kneel.

It is time for the invocation:

Kali, be with us.
Violence, destruction, receive our homage.
Help us to bring darkness into the light,
To lift out the pain, the anger,
Where it can be seen for what it is—
The balance-wheel for our vulnerable, aching love.
Put the wild hunger where it belongs,
Within the act of creation,
Crude power that forges a balance
Between hate and love.

Help us to be the always hopeful
Gardeners of the spirit
Who know that without darkness
Nothing comes to birth
As without light
Nothing flowers.

Bear the roots in mind,
You, the dark one, Kali,
Awesome power.

We have been struck by a lightning force
And roaring like beasts we have been caught
Exulting, bloody, glad to destroy and curse.
The tiger, violence, takes the human throat,

Glad of the blood, glad of the lust
In this jungle of action without will,
Where we can tear down what we hate at last.
That tiger strength—oh it is beautiful!

There is no effort. It is all success.
It feels like a glorious creation.
An absolute, it knows no more or less,
Cannot be worked at, is nothing but sensation.

That is its awful power, so like release
The animal within us roars its joy.
What other god could give us this wild peace
As we run out, tumultuous to destroy?

But when the tiger goes, we are alone,
Sleeping the madness off until some dawn
When human eyes wake, huge and forlorn,
To meet the human face that has been torn.

Who was a tiger once is weak and small,
And terribly unfit for all he has to do.
Lifting a single stone up from the rubble
Takes all his strength. And he hurts too.

Who is a friend here, who an enemy?
Each face he meets is the same savaged face
Recovering itself and marked by mystery.
There is no power left in this sad place—

Only the light of dawn and its cold shadow.
How place a cool hand on some burning head?
Even compassion is still dazed and raw.
The simplest gesture grates a way toward need.

After the violence peace does not rise
Like a forgiving sun to wash all clean,
Nor does it rush out like some fresh surmise
Without a thought for what the wars have been.

"I too am torn" or "Where is your hurt?"
The answer may be only silences.
The ghostly tiger lives on in the heart.
Wounds sometimes do not heal for centuries.

So the peace-maker must dig wells and build
Small shelters stone by stone, often afraid;
Must live with a long patience not to yield.
Only destruction wields a lightning blade.

After the tiger we become frail and human,
The dust of ruins acrid in the throat.
Oh brothers, take it as an absolution
That we must work so slowly toward hope!

"WE'LL TO THE WOODS NO MORE, THE LAURELS ARE CUT DOWN"
(*At Kent State*)

The war games are over,
The laurels all cut down.
We'll to the woods no more
With live ammunition
To murder our own children
Because they hated war.

The war games are over.
How many times in pain
We were given a choice—
"Sick of the violence"
(Oh passionate human voice!)—
But buried it again.

The war games are over.
Virile, each stood alone—
John, Robert, Martin Luther.
Still we invoke the gun,
Still make a choice for murder,
Bury the dead again.

The war games are over,
And all the laurel's gone.
Dead warrior, dead lover,
Was the war lost or won?
What say you, blasted head?
No answer from the dead.

NIGHT WATCH

Sweet night nursing a neighbor—
The old lady lifts her hands
And writes a message
On the air—
Gently I lay them down.
Sudden motion
Might shift the bandage
Over one eye.

Across the hall
A woman moans twice.
I alone am not in pain,
Wide-awake under a circle of light.

Two days ago in Kentucky
I was the sick child,
Sick for this patchy, barren earth,
For tart talk,
Dissatisfaction,
Sharp bitter laughter,
Sick for a granite pillow.

Among that grass soft as silk,
Those courtesies, those evasions,
I was sick as a trout
In a stagnant pond.

Wide-awake,
I weigh one thing against another.
The old lady will see
Better than before;
The woman who moaned
Sleeps herself whole again.

Sweet, innocent night
In the hospital
Where wounds can be healed!

The birds sing
Before dawn,
And before dawn
I begin to see a little.
I hold the old warm hand in mine
To keep it from clawing
The bandage,
And to comfort me.

I am happy as a mother
Whose good baby sleeps.

In Kentucky
They are spurned mothers,
Curse the children
And their hot black eyes,
Hard from not weeping;
Remember the old days,
Dear pickaninnies,
Mouths pink as watermelon.

What happens
When the baby screams,
Batters the barred cage of its bed,
Wears patience thin?

What happens
When the baby is six feet tall,
Throws stones,
Breaks windows?

What happens
When the grown man
Beats out against us
His own hard core,
Wants to hurt?

In the white night
At the hospital
I listened hard.

I weighed one thing
Against another.
I heard, "Love, love."
(Love them to death?)

And at dawn I heard a voice,
"If you love them,
Let them grow."

3

The convalescent
Is quick to weak rage
Or tears;
In a state of growth
We are in pain,
Violent, hard to live with.
Our wounds ache.
We curse rather than bless.

4

"I hate them," she said.
"They spoil everything," said
The woman from Baltimore.
"It is not the dear old town
I used to know."

I felt pain like an assault,
The old pain again
When the world thrusts itself inside,
When we have to take in the outside,
When we have to decide
To be crazy-human with hope
Or just plain crazy
With fear.

(The drunken Black in the subway
Will rape you, white woman,
Because you had bad dreams.)

Stomach pain, or vomit it.
In Kentucky I threw up

One whole night.
Get rid of this great sick baby
We carry around
Or go through the birth-sweat again.
Lazy heart,
Slow self-indulgent beat,
Take the sick world in.

5

In Baltimore
The Black who drove me to the airport
Seemed an enormous, touchable
Blessing.
"When you give a speech," he told me,
"And you get that scared feeling,
Take a deep breath. It helps."

Comfort flowed out from him.
He talked about pain
In terms of healing.
Of Baltimore, that great hospital
Where the wounds fester
Among azaleas and dogwood,
The lovely quiet gardens,
"We are making things happen,"
Said the black man.
"It is going to be beautiful."
He had no doubt.

Wide awake in the hospital
In the morning light,
I weighed one thing against the other.
I took a deep breath.

Part Two

PROTEUS

They were intense people, given to migraine,
Outbursts of arrogance, self-pity, or wild joy,
Affected by the weather like a weathervane,
Hungry for glory, exhausted by each day,
Humble at night and filled with self-distrust.
Time burned their heels. They ran because they must—

Sparkled, spilled over in the stress of living.
Oh, they were fickle, fluid, sometimes cruel,
Who still imagined they were always giving;
And the mind burned experience like fuel,
So they were sovereign losers, clumsy winners,
And read the saints, and knew themselves as sinners.

Wild blood subdued, it was pure form they blest.
Their sunlit landscapes were painted across pain.
They dreamed of peaceful gardens and of rest—
And now their joys, their joys alone remain.
Transparent, smiling, like calm gods to us,
Their names are Mozart, Rilke—Proteus.

A LAST WORD
(for my students at Wellesley College)

Whatever we found in that room was not easy,
But harder and harder, and for me as well,
Fumbling for words when what we fumbled for
Could not be spoken, the crude source itself;
The clever people had no news to tell.

The best failed. That is the way it is.
The best knew what we were mining after
Was not to be reached or counted in an hour.
The worst poems, maybe, became fertile,
And we knew moments of pure crazy laughter.

Often you came into that room becalmed,
Your faces buttoned against the afternoon.
If the hour occasionally opened into trees,
If we digressed, leaving the subject flat,
Well, we were fighting hard against the gloom.

The vivid battle brought us within the hour
Out of the doldrums together, edged and warm.
At any instant the fall of a mask
Released some naked wisdom; an open face
Surprised itself and took our world by storm.

For you, I trust, the time was never wasted;
For me, driven to dig deep under my cover,
Into the unsafe places where poets operate,
There is no grief; too much was taken and given,
More than administrators can discover.

And so you go your ways, and I go mine,
Yours into the world at last, and mine away—
To some adventure on another planet.
Whatever failed or you still hoped to do
Will grow to harvest in some other way,

Not against the stream of a college, but
Toward an ordering of the spirit in pure air

Where no one is bound by custom, or so engined
Toward immediate goals, and trapped by time:
Your poems will happen when no one is there.

And when the angel comes, you will remember
Our fierce encounter, beyond devious ways,
Not at the end of some blank corridor—
Outside all walls, the daring spirit's wrench
To open up a simple world of praise!

GIRL WITH 'CELLO

There had been no such music here until
A girl came in from falling dark and snow
To bring into this house her glowing 'cello
As if some silent, magic animal.

She sat, head bent, her long hair all a-spill
Over the breathing wood, and drew the bow.
There had been no such music here until
A girl came in from falling dark and snow.

And she drew out that sound so like a wail,
A rich dark suffering joy, as if to show
All that a wrist holds and that fingers know
When they caress a magic animal.
There had been no such music here until
A girl came in from falling dark and snow.

AN INTRUDER

The other day a witch came to call.
She brought a basket full of woe and gall
And left it there for me in my front hall.

But it was empty when I found it there
And she herself had gone back to her lair
Leaving the bats of rage to fly my air.

Out of ambivalence this witch was born;
All that she gives is subtly smeared and torn
Or slightly withered by her love and scorn.

The furies sit and watch me as I write;
The bats fly silently about all night
And a black mist obscures the kindest light.

But I shall find the magic note to play,
Or, like a donkey, learn the wild flat bray
That sends all furies howling on their way.

The note is laughter. No witch could withstand
The frightful joke all witches understand
When they are given all that they demand.

The word can neither bless nor curse, of course.
It must bewitch a witch and leave her worse.
Perhaps I'll call her just a failed old nurse.

Love cannot exorcize the gifts of hate.
Hate cannot exorcize what has no weight,
But laughter we can never over-rate.

THE MUSE AS MEDUSA

I saw you once, Medusa; we were alone.
I looked you straight in the cold eye, cold.
I was not punished, was not turned to stone—
How to believe the legends I am told?

I came as naked as any little fish,
Prepared to be hooked, gutted, caught;
But I saw you, Medusa, made my wish,
And when I left you I was clothed in thought . . .

Being allowed, perhaps, to swim my way
Through the great deep and on the rising tide,
Flashing wild streams, as free and rich as they,
Though you had power marshalled on your side.

The fish escaped to many a magic reef;
The fish explored many a dangerous sea—
The fish, Medusa, did not come to grief,
But swims still in a fluid mystery.

Forget the image: your silence is my ocean,
And even now it teems with life. You chose
To abdicate by total lack of motion,
But did it work, for nothing really froze?

It is all fluid still, that world of feeling
Where thoughts, those fishes, silent, feed and rove;
And, fluid, it is also full of healing,
For love is healing, even rootless love.

I turn your face around! It is my face.
That frozen rage is what I must explore—
Oh secret, self-enclosed, and ravaged place!
This is the gift I thank Medusa for.

FOR ROSALIND
On Her Seventy-fifth Birthday

Tonight we come to praise
Her splendor, not her years,
Pure form and what it burns—
Who teaches this or learns?—
Intrinsic, beyond tears,
Splendor that has no age.
Take your new-fangled beauties off the stage!

The high poise of the throat
That dazzled every heart—
Who was not young and awed
By beauty so unflawed
It seemed not life, but art?—
Terrible as a swan
Young children, deeply moved, might look upon.

The blazing sapphire eyes—
They looked out from a queen.
Yet there was wildness near;
She glimmered like a deer
No hunter could bring down.
So warm, so wild, so proud,
She moved among us like a light-brimmed cloud.

The way her dresses flowed!
So once in Greece, so once . . .
Passion and its control.
She drew many a soul
To join her in the dance.
Give homage fierce as rage.
Take your new-fangled beauties off the stage!

THE GREAT TRANSPARENCIES

Lately I have been thinking much of those,
The open ones, the great transparencies,
Through whom life—is it wind or water?—flows
Unstinted, who have learned the sovereign ease.
They are not young; they are not ever young.

Youth is too vulnerable to bear the tide,
And let it rise, and never hold it back,
Then let it ebb, not suffering from pride,
Nor thinking it must ebb from private lack.
The elders yield because they are so strong—

Seized by the great wind like a ripening field,
All rippled over in a sensuous sweep,
Wave after wave, lifted and glad to yield,
But whether wind or water, never keep
The tide from flowing or hold it back for long.

Lately I have been thinking much of these,
The unafraid although still vulnerable,
Through whom life flows, the great transparencies,
The old and open, brave and beautiful . . .
They are not young; they are not ever young.

FRIENDSHIP: THE STORMS

How much you have endured of storm
Among sweet summer flowers!
The black hail falls so hard to do us harm
In my dark hours,

Though friendship is not quick to burn,
It is explosive stuff;
The edge of our awareness is so keen
A word is enough.

Clouds rise up from the blue
And darken the sky,
And we are tossed about from false to true
Not knowing why.

After this violence is over
I turn my life, my art,
Round and around to discover
The fault in my heart—

What breeds this cruel weather,
Why tensions grow;
And when we have achieved so much together,
What breaks the flow.

God help us, friendship is aware
That where we fail we learn;
Tossed on a temperament, I meet you there
At every turn.

In this kaleidoscope
Of work and complex living,
For years you buttressed and enlivened hope,
Laid balm on grieving.

After the angry cloud has broken
I know what you are—
How love renews itself, spoken, unspoken,
Cool as the morning star.

EVENING WALK IN FRANCE

When twilight comes, before it gets too late,
We swing behind us the heavy iron gate,

And as it clangs shut, stand a moment there
To taste the world, the larger open air,

And walk among the grandeur of the vines,
Those long rows written in imperfect lines,

Low massive trunks that bear the delicate
Insignia of leaves where grapes are set;

And here the sky is a great roofless room
Where late bees and late people wander home,

And here we walk on slowly through the dusk
And watch the long waves of the dark that mask

Black cypresses far off, and gently take
The sumptuous clouds and roofs within their wake,

Until the solid nearer haystacks seem
Like shadows looming ghostly out of dream,

And the stone farm becomes an ancient lair,
Dissolving into dusk—and is not there.

A dog barks, and a single lamp is lit.
We are two silent shadows crossing it.

Under the lamp a woman stands at rest,
Cutting a loaf of bread across her breast.

DUTCH INTERIOR
Pieter de Hooch (1629–1682)

I recognize the quiet and the charm,
This safe enclosed room where a woman sews
And life is tempered, orderly, and calm.

Through the Dutch door, half open, sunlight streams
And throws a pale square down on the red tiles.
The cosy black dog suns himself and dreams.

Even the bed is sheltered, it encloses,
A cupboard to keep people safe from harm,
Where copper glows with the warm flush of roses.

The atmosphere is all domestic, human,
Chaos subdued by the sheer power of need.
This is a room where I have lived as woman,

Lived too what the Dutch painter does not tell—
The wild skies overhead, dissolving, breaking,
And how that broken light is never still,

And how the roar of waves is always near,
What bitter tumult, treacherous and cold,
Attacks the solemn charm year after year!

It must be felt as peace won and maintained
Against those terrbile antagonists—
How many from this quiet room have drowned?

How many left to go, drunk on the wind,
And take their ships into heartbreaking seas;
How many whom no woman's peace could bind?

Bent to her sewing, she looks drenched in calm.
Raw grief is disciplined to the fine thread.
But in her heart this woman is the storm;

Alive, deep in herself, holds wind and rain,
Remaking chaos into an intimate order
Where sometimes light flows through a windowpane.

A VISION OF HOLLAND

The marriage of this horizontal land
Lying so low, so open and exposed,
Flat as an open palm, and never closed
To restless storm and the relentless wind,

This marriage of low land and towering air—
It took my breath away. I am still crazed
Here, a month later, in my uplands, dazed
By so much light, so close to despair.

Infinite vertical! Who climbs to Heaven?
Who can assault the cloud's shimmering peak?
Here the intangible is the mystique,
No rock to conquer and no magic mountain,

Only the horizontal infinite
Stretched there below to polarize
The rush of height itself, where this land lies
Immense and still, covered by changing light.

Those troubling clouds pour through the mind.
An earthquake of pure atmosphere
Cracks open every elemental fear.
The light is passionate, but not defined.

So we are wracked as by a psychic fault,
Stormed and illuminated. "Oh sky, sky,
Earth, earth, and nothing else," we cry,
Knowing once more how absolutes exalt.

Slowly the eye comes back again to rest
There on a house, canal, cows in a field.
The visionary moment has to yield,
But the defining eye is newly blest.

Come back from that cracked-open psychic place,
It is alive to wonders freshly seen:
After the earthquake, gentle pastures green,
And that great miracle, a human face.

Part Three

Kind kinderpark
For bear buffoons
And fluid graces—
Who dreamed this lark
Of spouts, lagoons,
And huge fur faces?

For bears designed
Small nooks, great crags,
And Gothic mountains?
For bears refined
Delightful snags,
Waterfalls, fountains?

Who had the wit to root
A forked tree where a sack
Of honey plumps on end,
A rich-bottomed fruit
To rouse a hearty whack
From passing friend?

Who ever did imagine
A waterspout as stool,
Or was black bear the wiser
Who sat down on this engine
To keep a vast rump cool,
Then, cooled, set free a geyser?

Who dreamed a great brown queen
Sleeked down in her rough silk
Flirting with her huge lord,
Breast-high in her tureen?—
"Splash me, delightful hulk!"
So happy and absurd.

Bear upside-down, white splendor,
All creamy, foaming fur,
And childhood's rug come true,

All nonchalance and candor,
Black pads your signature—
Who, above all, dreamed you?

When natural and formal
Are seen to mate so well,
Where bears and fountains play,
Who would return to normal?
Go back to human Hell?
Not I. I mean to stay,

To hold this happy chance
Forever in the mind,
To be where waters fall
And archetypes still dance,
As they were once designed
In Eden for us all.

A PARROT

My parrot is emerald green,
His tail feathers, marine.
He bears an orange half-moon
Over his ivory beak.
He must be believed to be seen,
This bird from a Rousseau wood.
When the urge is on him to speak,
He becomes too true to be good.

He uses his beak like a hook
To lift himself up with or break
Open a sunflower seed,
And his eye, in a bold white ring,
Has a lapidary look.
What a most astonishing bird,
Whose voice when he chooses to sing
Must be believed to be heard.

That stuttered staccato scream
Must be believed not to seem
The shriek of a witch in the room.
But he murmurs some muffled words
(Like someone who talks through a dream)
When he sits in the window and sees
The to-and-fro wings of wild birds
In the leafless improbable trees.

FROGS AND PHOTOGRAPHERS

The temperamental frog,
A loving expert says,
Exhibits stimulation
By rolling of bright eyes
(This is true frog-elation);
But in a different mood
Withdraws under a leaf
Or simulated bog
(This is frog's sign of grief),
Closes his eyes to brood.
Frogs do not weep, they hide.

The camera makes him cross.
Eyes glaze or tightly close;
His whole expression's changed.
He will not take a pose,
He has become estranged
Who was so bright and gay—
"Hysterical," they say,
As subject, total loss—
Burrows himself away,
Will not rise to a fly:
The frog is camera-shy.

A form of lunacy?
But whose face does not freeze,
Eyes shut or wildly blink?
Who does not sometimes sneeze
Just at the camera's wink?
Withdraw to worlds inside?
Invent himself a bog?
And more neurotic we
Than the spontaneous frog,
Sometimes cannot decide
Whether to weep or hide.

EINE KLEINE SNAILMUSIK

"The snail watchers are interested in snails from all angles.
. . . At the moment they are investigating the snail's reaction to
music. 'We have played to them on the harp in the garden and
in the country on the pipe,' said Mr. Heaton, 'and we have taken
them into the house and played to them on the piano.'"

—*The London Star*

What soothes the angry snail?
What's music to his horn?
For the "Sonata Appassionata,"
He shows scorn,
And Handel
Makes the frail snail
Quail,
While Prokofieff
Gets no laugh,
And Tchaikovsky, I fear,
No tear.
Piano, pipe, and harp,
Dulcet or shrill,
Flat or sharp,
Indoors or in the garden,
Are willy-nilly
Silly
To the reserved, slow,
Sensitive
Snail,
Who prefers to live
Glissandissimo,
Pianissimo.

THE FIG

Under the green leaf hangs a little pouch
Shaped like a gourd, purple and leathery.
It fits the palm, it magnetizes touch.
What flesh designed as fruit can this fruit be?

The plump skin gives a little at the seam.
Now bite it deep for better or for worse!
Oh multitude of stars, pale green and crimson—
And you have dared to eat a universe!

HAWAIIAN PALM

Being ourselves still earthbound,
All we see in the beginning
Is tree rooted, tree from the ground,
That tensile gray trunk just leaning
(Literal, stiff, a little off-plumb)
Over the lazy purple and greening
Of waves on the coral honeycomb.

From here our wandering eyes mount
Slowly to its surprising head,
A baroque casque, a great fount
Of spiny plumes that tremble their load,—
See first panache against flat blue,
And only later under this shade
The clutch of rich ovarian fruit.

The tree is separated essence,
First rooted, then fruitful, standing
Unmoved, it would seem, and tense.
We do not catch the subtle blending
Until we are bored, half in trance,
Able to sense the ever-spending
Rich presence as a dance.

Vision, airborne, is shifted slightly
To watch the singing mind in motion.
Wind plays the pleated leaves so sweetly
Form is not broken; silence is seen,
A shimmer, a music for the eye;
And now we penetrate all sheen
To wisdom, rooted, dancing lightly.

Part Four

A HARD DEATH

We have seen how dignity can be torn
From the naked dying or the newly born
By a loud voice or an ungentle presence,
Harshness of haste or lack of reverence;
How the hospital nurse may casually unbind
The suffering body from the lucid mind.
The spirit enclosed in that fragile shell
Cannot defend itself, must endure all.
And not only the dying, helpless in a bed,
Ask for a little pillow for the head,
A sip of water, a cool hand to bless:
The living have their lonely agonies.
"Is there compassion?" a friend asked me.
"Does it exist in another country?"

The busy living have no time to see
The flowers, so silent and so alive,
That paling to lavender of the anemone,
That purpling of the rose no one can save,
Dying, but at each second so complete
A photograph would show no slightest change.
Only the human eye, imperfect but aware,
Knows that the flower arrested on the air
Is flying through space, doing a dance
Toward the swift fall of petals, all at once.

God's Grace, given freely, we do not deserve,
But we can choose at least to see its ghost
On every face. Oh, we can wish to serve
Each other gently as we live, though lost.
We cannot save, be saved, but we can stand
Before each presence with gentle heart and hand;
Here in this place, in this time without belief,
Keep the channels open to each other's grief;
Never accept a death or life as strange
To its essence, but at each second be aware

How God is moving always through each flower
From birth to death in a multiple gesture
Of abnegation; and when the petals fall
Say it is beautiful and good, say it is well.

I saw my mother die and now I know
The spirit cannot be defended. It must go
Naked even of love at the very end.
"Take the flowers away" (Oh, she had been their friend!),
And we who ached could do nothing more—
She was detached and distant as a star.

Let us be gentle to each other this brief time
For we shall die in exile far from home,
Where even the flowers can no longer save.
Only the living can be healed by love.

THE SILENCE

At first the silence is a silence only,
A huge lack rather than a huge something.
I listen for a voice in this dead vacuum,
Feel destitute, abandoned, full of dread.

Season of growing light and dirty snow
When we are too vulnerable for words.

The silence—at first it is empty.
Tears fall out of my eyes like falling leaves.
To whom, to what is it goodbye? Such grief.
At first the silence is a silence only.

Season of separation and the winter freeze.
Only the skies are open these hard days.

The brooks are numbed inside their caves of ice.
Who knows—who can?—what is in store for us?
Our dying planet where the glazed fields shine—
No gentle snow falls in this cruel time.

Silence, a membrane. Somehow I must get through
Into the universe where stars still flock,
To the rich world not empty but wide open,
Where soul quietly breathes and is at home.

First, I must go beyond the loneliness,
Refuse dependence and not ask for love.

So I went up the hill with my raw grief,
Found lambs there, shivering, newly born.
The sheep's gruff voice, anxious, as she licked one,
Repeated a hoarse word, a word torn from her,

I had never heard that sound before—
That throaty cry of hunger and arrival.

Oh yes, I nearly drowned with longing then . . .
Now winter hills surround me in the evening light.

A dying sun, cold sky flushed with rose
Speak of the separation in all birth.

At first the silence is a silence only . . .
But huge lack bears huge something through the dark.

ANNUNCIATION

In this suspense of ours before the fall,
Before the end, before the true beginning,
No word, no feeling can be pure or whole.
Bear the loss first, then the infant winning;
Agony first, and then the long farewell.
So the child leaves the parent torn at birth.
No one is perfect here, no one is well:
It is a time of fear and immolation.
First the hard journey down again to death
Without a saving word or a free breath,
And then the terrible annunciation:
And we are here alone upon the earth.

The angel comes and he is always grave.
Joy is announced as if it were despair.
Mary herself could do nothing to save,
Nothing at all but to believe and bear,
Nothing but to foresee that in the ending
Would lie the true beginning and the birth,
And all be broken down before the mending.
For there can never be annunciation
Without the human heart's descent to Hell.
And no ascension without the fearful fall.
The angel's wings foretold renunciation,
And left her there alone upon the earth.

AT CHARTRES

Perhaps there is no smallest consolation,
No help, no saving grace, no little ease;
Only the presence of this pure compassion
We lifted up, who fall upon our knees.
Nothing we have to give it or implore.
It does not speak to us. It has no face,
And is itself only an open door—
Forever open, that will never close.

Here we are measured by our own creation.
Against this little anguish, this short breath,
Those choirs of glass rise up in an ovation,
Ourselves so small, this house so huge with faith.
Here we are measured against the perfect love,
Transparent glowing walls define and free.
The door is open, but we cannot move,
Nor be consoled or saved. But only see.

ONCE MORE AT CHARTRES

A desperate child, I run up to this gate
With all my fears withheld and all my dark
Contained, to breathe out in one breath
All I have carried in my heart of death,
All I have buried in my mind of hate.
Once more I stand within the ancient ark.

> Chartres, you are here who never will not be,
> Ever becoming what you always are.
> So, lifted by our human eyes, each hour,
> The arch is breathed alive into its power,
> Still being builded for us who still see
> Hands lifting stone into the perilous air.

A child, I rest in your maternal gaze,
That which encompasses and shelters, yet,
Lifting so gently, still demands re-birth,
Breaks open toward sky the dark of earth,
And proves unyielding where the rose is set,
Where Love is light itself and severe praise.

> Chartres, you the reason beyond any faith,
> The prayer we make who never learned to pray,
> The patient recreator of creation,
> O distant friend, O intimate relation,
> You living seed in the disease of death,
> And long becoming of our only day,

I stand within your arduous embrace.
This is pure majesty, there is no other.
I suffer all beginnings and all ends.
Here this enclosure opens and transcends
All weaker hopes under your tragic face—
The suffering child here must become the mother.

JONAH

I come back from the belly of the whale
Bruised from the struggle with a living wall,
Drowned in a breathing dark, a huge heart-beat
That jolted helpless hands and useless feet,

Yet know it was not death, that vital warm,
Nor did the monster wish me any harm;
Only the prisoning was hard to bear
And three-weeks' need to burst back into air . .

Slowly the drowned self must be strangled free
And lifted whole out of that inmost sea,
To lie newborn under compassionate sky,
As fragile as a babe, with welling eye.

Do not be anxious, for now all is well,
The sojourn over in that fluid Hell,
My heart is nourished on no more than air,
Since every breath I draw is answered prayer.

EASTER MORNING

The extreme delicacy of this Easter morning
Spoke to me as a prayer and as a warning.
It was light on the brink, spring light
After a rain that gentled my dark night.
I walked through landscapes I had never seen
Where the fresh grass had just begun to green,
And its roots, watered deep, sprung to my tread;
The maples wore a cloud of feathery red,
But flowering trees still showed their clear design
Against the pale blue brightness chilled like wine.
And I was praying all the time I walked,
While starlings flew about, and talked, and talked.
Somewhere and everywhere life spoke the word.
The dead trees woke; each bush held its bird.
I prayed for delicate love and difficult,
That all be gentle now and know no fault,
That all be patient—as a wild rabbit fled
Sudden before me. Dear love, I would have said
(And to each bird who flew up from the wood),
I would be gentler still if that I could,
For on this Easter morning it would seem
The softest footfall danger is, extreme . . .
And so I prayed to be less than the grass
And yet to feel the Presence that might pass.
I made a prayer. I heard the answer, "Wait,
When all is so in peril, and so delicate!"

THE GODHEAD AS LYNX

Kyrie Eleison, O wild lynx!
Mysterious sad eyes, and yet so bright,
Wherein mind never grieves or thinks,
But absolute attention is alight—
Before that golden gaze, so deep and cold,
My human rage dissolves, my pride is broken.
I am a child here in a world grown old.
Eons ago its final word was spoken.
Eyes of the god, hard as obsidian,
Look into mine. Kyrie Eleison.

Terrible as it is, your gaze consoles,
And awe turns tender before your guiltless head.
(What we have lost to enter into souls!)
I feel a longing for the lynx's bed,
To submerge self in that essential fur,
And sleep close to this ancient world of grace,
As if there could be healing next to her,
The mother-lynx in her pre-human place.
Yet that pure beauty does not know compassion—
O cruel god, Kyrie Eleison!

It is the marvelous world, free of our love,
Free of our hate, before our own creation,
Animal world, so still and so alive.
We never can go back to pure sensation,
Be self-possessed as the great lynx, or calm.
Yet she is lightning to cut down the lamb,
A beauty that devours without a qualm,
A cruel god who only says, "I am,"
Never, "You must become," as you, our own
God say forever. Kyrie Eleison!

How rarely You look out from human eyes,
Yet it is we who bear creation on,
Troubled, afflicted, and so rarely wise,
Feeling nostalgia for an old world gone.

Imperfect as we are, and never whole,
Still You live in us like a fertile seed,
Always becoming, and asking of the soul
To stretch beyond sweet nature, answer need,
And lay aside the beauty of the lynx
To be this laboring self who groans and thinks.

THE WAVES

Even in the middle of the silent firs,
The secret world of mushroom and of moss,
Where all is delicate and nothing stirs,
We get the rumor of those distant wars
And the harsh sound of loss.

This is an island open to the churning,
The boom, the constant cannonade,
The turning back of tides and their returning,
And ocean broken like some restless mourning
That cannot find a bed.

Oh love, let us be true then to this will—
Not to each other, human and defeated,
But to great power, our Heaven and our Hell,
That thunders out its triumph unabated,
And is never still.

For we are married to this rocky coast,
To the charge of huge waves upon it,
The ceaseless war, the tide gained and then lost,
And ledges worn down smooth but not downcast—
Wild rose and granite.

Here in the darkness of the stillest wood,
Absence, the ocean, tires us with its roar;
We bear love's thundering rumor in the blood
Beyond our understanding, ill or good—
Listen, once more!

BEYOND THE QUESTION

1

The phoebe sits on her nest
Hour after hour,
Day after day,
Waiting for life to burst out
From under her warmth.

Can I weave a nest for silence,
Weave it of listening,
Listening,
Layer upon layer?

But one must first become small,
Nothing but a presence,
Attentive as a nesting bird,
Proffering no slightest wish,
No tendril of a wish
Toward anything that might happen
Or be given,
Only the warm, faithful waiting,
Contained in one's smallness.

Beyond the question, the silence.
Before the answer, the silence.

2

When all is in order,
Flowers on each mantel,
Floors swept,
Newspapers laid aside,
Wars, deaths suspended . . .
Silence flows in
And it happens—
A patch of sunlight
On the wall, a message;
The great white peony,

An illumination.
Each thing is haloed.
I live in a Book of Hours.

3

Before my eyes the peony,
An arrested whirlpool,
Soft as the breast of a swan,
Floats on the air . . .

Before my eyes,
The petals fall apart,
Plop down
In shapeless confusion,
The pure form spent.

Creation itself
Tears the fabric apart,
In the instant of achievement
Makes new demands.

Must I rejoice
In the harsh, fertile
Answer to loss,
The stiff, five-pointed seed?

Not keep it
A moment longer,
Magic floating on air,
The flower,
The fulfillment?

No, creation says,
Not a moment longer.

4

Voices do not speak
From a cloud.
They breathe through the blood.
They are there in the stem
(Plant or human flesh).

Does the seed too resist?
But something cracks the shell,
Breaks down the pod,
Explodes
That dark enclosed life,
Safe, self-contained,
Pushes the frail root out,
The fresh dangerous leaf.

Voices do not speak
From a cloud,
But we are inhabited.

5

Now at last
The dialogue begins again.
I lay my cheek on the hard earth
And listen, listen.

No, it is not the endless conversations
Of the grasses and their shallow roots;
No, it is not the beetles,
The good worms, I hear,
But tremor much deeper down.

Answer?
But the answer is happening,
Flows through every crevice
And across the stillest air.
Under the ledges
Artesian water
Flows fast
Even in time of drought.

INVOCATION

Come out of the dark earth
Here where the minerals
Glow in their stone cells
Deeper than seed or birth.

Come under the strong wave
Here where the tug goes
As the tide turns and flows
Below that architrave.

Come into the pure air
Above all heaviness
Of storm and cloud to this
Light-possessed atmosphere.

Come into, out of, under
The earth, the wave, the air.
Love, touch us everywhere
With primeval candor.

MAY SARTON

Born in Belgium and educated in the United States, May Sarton is the daughter of George Sarton, the distinguished historian of science and Mabel Elwes Sarton, an artist. She has studied, performed and taught the theater arts, but is best known for her work as a poet and a novelist. She has traveled widely all over the world, and taught in numerous universities in this country. She has had over twenty books published, including her two recent volumes of poetry: Cloud, Stone, Sun, Vine *(1961) and* A Private Mythology *(1966). She now lives in an old house in a small New Hampshire village.*